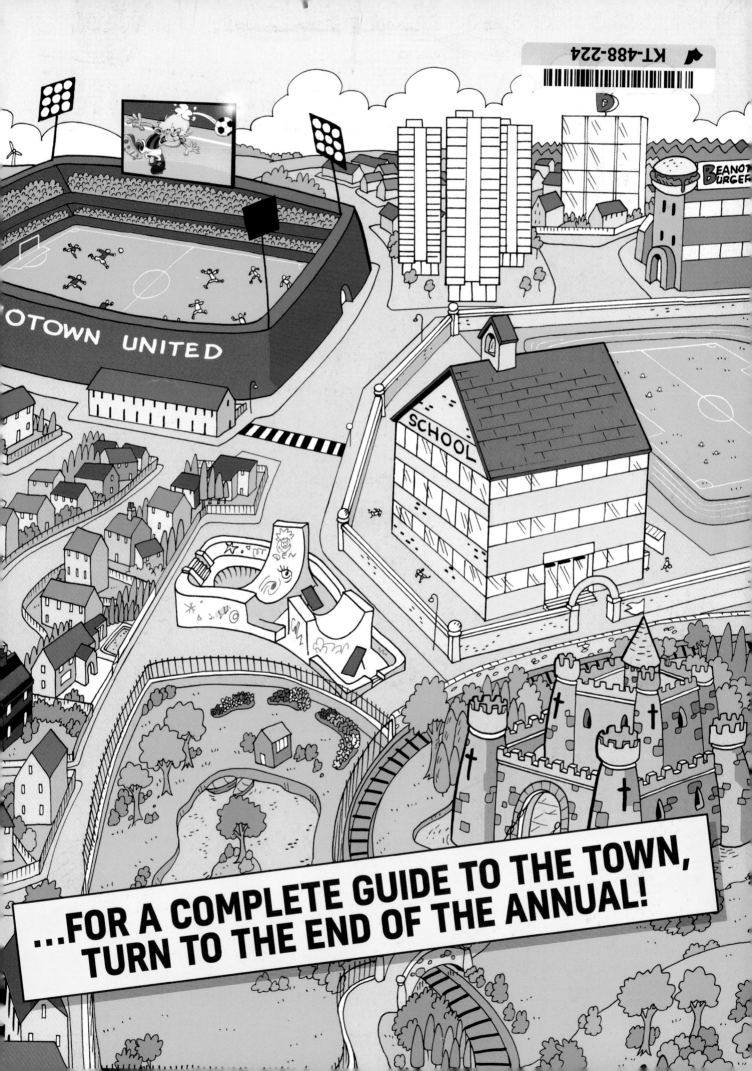

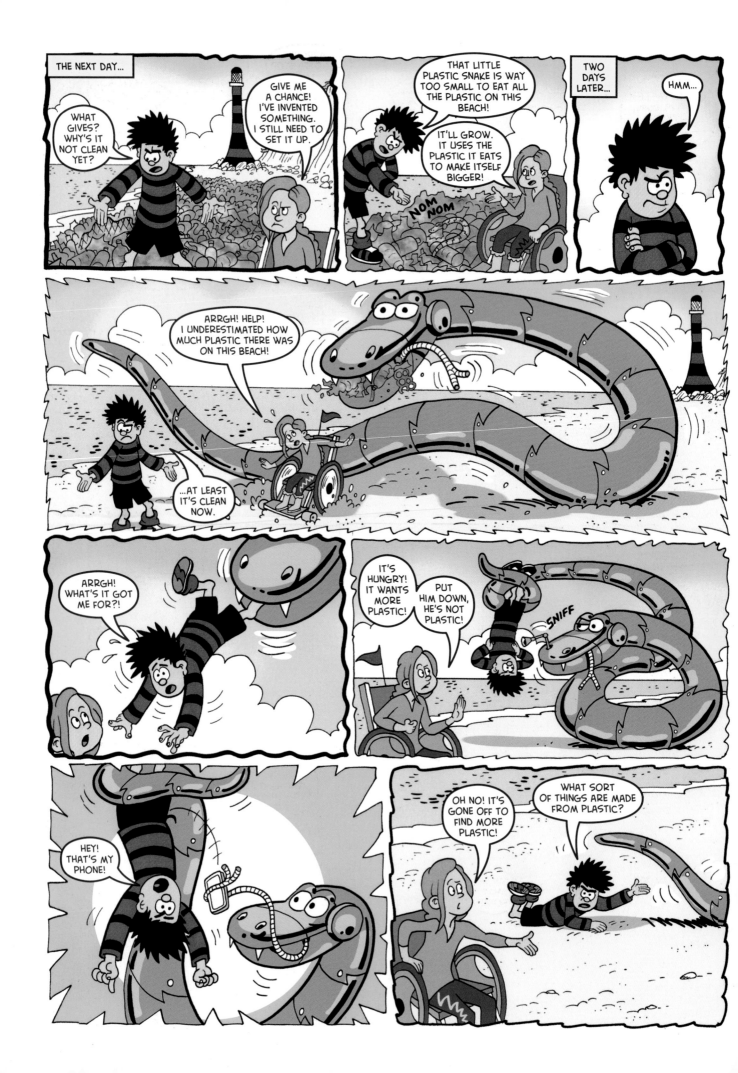

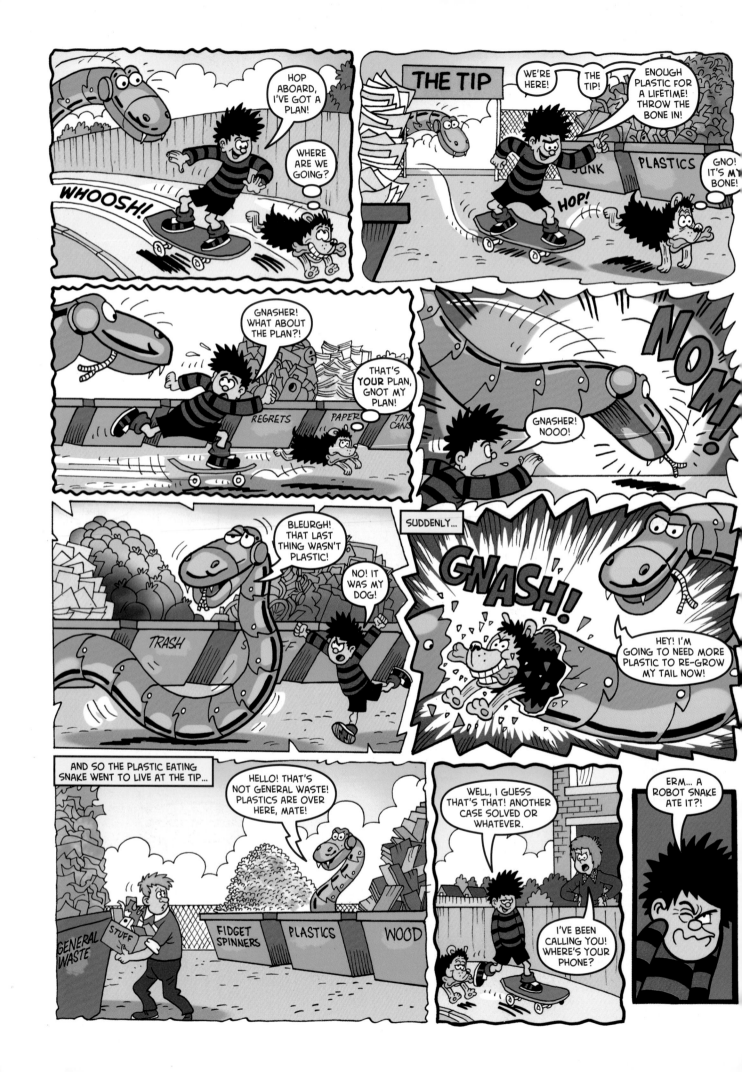

THE BASH STREET KIDS

THE CLASS EVERY TEACHER DREADS...

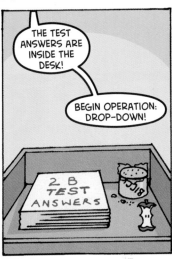

DANGEROUS DAN!
BEANOTOWN'S TOP SECRET AGENT!

Diary of a Prankster

By Tricky Dicky aged 8¼

PRANK No. 1

YOU'LL NEED:
- Pepper
- A sunflower

Dear Diary,
This prank will really make people stop and smell the flowers! Or not!

1 Choose a nice sunflower.

2 Shake lots of pepper over the brown centre of the sunflower.

AAH...

3 Ask someone to smell it.

...CHOO!

4 When they take a whiff, they'll sneeze worse than when they get hay fever!

BETTY AND THE YETI!

THE ORDINARY GIRL WITH THE EXTRAORDINARY BEST FRIEND!

YETI HUNGRY!

YOU'RE ALWAYS HUNGRY, YETI!

HEY! HERE'S A WAY YOU CAN EAT LOTS FOR FREE!

HOT DOG EATING CONTEST TODAY!

IS IT TOO LATE TO ENTER MY, ER... COUSIN AGNES?

S-S-SIGN HERE, YOUNG LADY!

ON YOUR MARKS... GET SET... SCOFF!

NOM!

MORE HOT DOGS!

NUM!

IT LOOKS LIKE WE HAVE A CLEAR WINNER! CONTESTANT NUMBER 9, AGNES!

MORE HOT DOGS?

AGNES WINS THE COVETED GOLD HOT DOG! JUST REMEMBER TO RETURN IT FOR NEXT YEAR'S...

NOM!

ER... HEH-HEH! LET'S GO, AGNES!

I CAN'T TAKE YOU ANYWHERE, CAN I?

YETI HUNGRY!

RUBI'S SCREWTOP SCIENCE

RUBIDIUM! WHAT ON EARTH DO YOU THINK YOU'RE DOING IN HERE?

I'M CONVERTING THIS CHRISTMAS JUMPER INTO A **DIMENSION JUMPER** SO WE CAN LEAP BETWEEN DIMENSIONS!

NO WAY, RUBIDIUM! ONE WRONG CALCULATION AND YOU COULD UNDO THE VERY **FABRIC** OF THE UNIVERSE!

BUT LOOK HOW AWESOME IT IS, DAD!

NOT TO MENTION THE DAMAGE YOU COULD DO TO THE FABRIC OF THAT JUMPER!

HAVE YOU EVER TRIED GETTING INTERDIMENSIONAL PARTICLES OUT OF **WOOL**? IT'S IMPOSSIBLE!

BAH!

NO MORE MEDDLING WITH PARALLEL UNIVERSES! AND THAT'S MY **FINAL WORD**!

YOUR DAD SOUNDED PRETTY MAD, RUBI!

WELL, HE IS A DAD. I'M PRETTY SURE IT'S IN THE JOB DESCRIPTION. HMM... WHY WON'T THIS THING WORK?

CAN I WARM UP MY PIE IN YOUR MICROWAVE? I'M STARVING!

MICROWAVE?

THAT'S NOT A MICROWAVE! THAT'S THE QUANTUM ACCELERATOR!

PING!

PAFF!

WHOA! WHAT HAPPENED?

ACCORDING TO THIS, WE DID IT! WE'VE LEAPT INTO **ANOTHER DIMENSION**!

WE'RE THE FIRST PEOPLE TO HAVE SUCCESSFULLY TRAVELLED INTO A PARALLEL UNIVERSE!

PIES STILL TASTE DELICIOUS IN THIS DIMENSION! CHOMP!

WHO KNOWS WHAT WE'LL FIND OUTSIDE THESE DOORS?

OUTSIDE...

HERE COMES YOUR DAD – AND HE DOESN'T LOOK HAPPY!

THIS IS DISAPPOINTING – IT ALL LOOKS THE SAME!

RUBIDIUM! I NEED TO HAVE A WORD WITH YOU, YOUNG LADY.

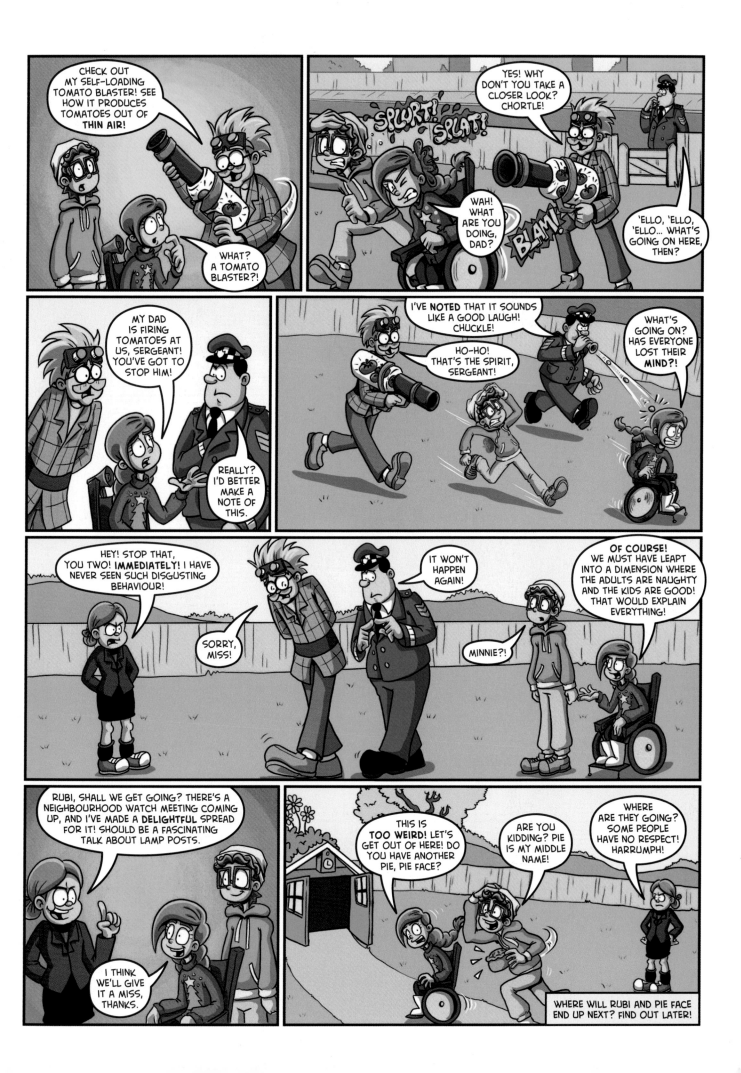

BILLY WHIZZ
THE FASTEST BOY IN THE WORLD!

BILLY'S SO EXCITED ABOUT THE CIRCUS COMING TO TOWN TODAY, HE'S BEEN FIDGETING IN HIS BED ALL NIGHT!

ER... SO WHERE IS HE? – ED

HERE I AM!

MY WHIZZ-FIDGETING WORE A HOLE STRAIGHT THROUGH THE BED!

MUST SEE IF THE CIRCUS IS HERE YET!

ARE YOU THE CIRCUS?

YES, BUT IT'S ONLY 6AM. WE HAVEN'T EVEN PUT UP THE BIG TOP YET!

CIRCUS

I'LL DO IT FOR YOU AT WHIZZ-SPEED!

VERY IMPRESSIVE!

I BET IT LOOKS AWESOME INSIDE!

OOF! I PUT IT UP SO FAST, I DIDN'T REALISE I'D PUT IT UP OVER A MARSH!

HAW-HAW!

AFTER BILLY HAS RE-ERECTED THE TENT...

CAN I BE IN THE SHOW? I'VE BEEN PRACTISING MY CIRCUS SKILLS!

WELL, SINCE YOU HELPED US... WHAT CAN YOU DO?

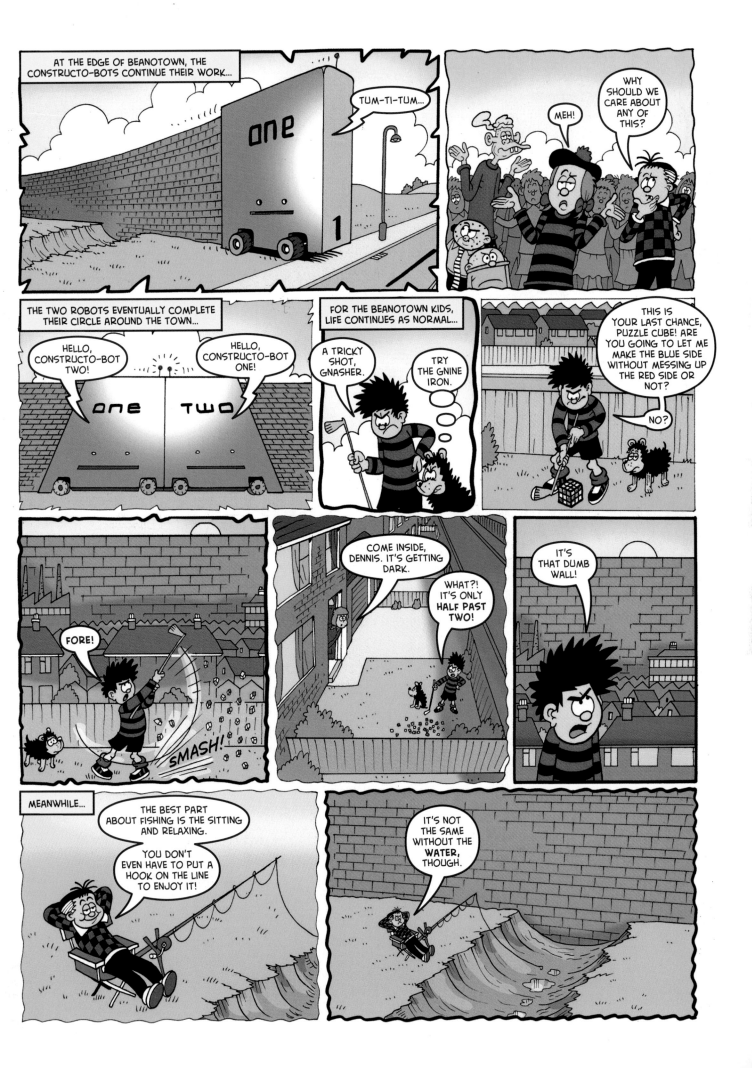

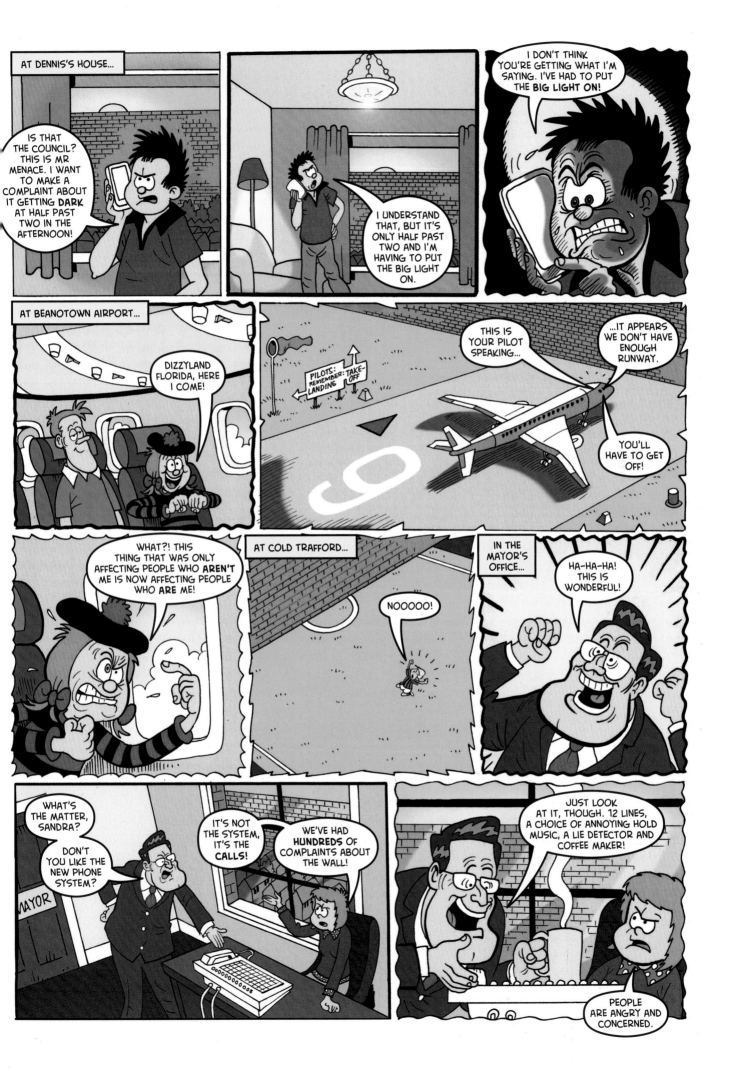

MINNIE THE MINX
SHE'S TOUGHER THAN ALL THE BOYS...

HEY, FRANCIS. WANNA DO SOMETHING AWESOME?

I WISH! I'VE ALREADY SPENT THIS WEEK'S POCKET MONEY. I'M SKINT!

ME TOO. WE NEED TO MAKE SOME CASH!

HOW ARE WE GOING TO DO THAT?

OOH, LOOK. ZOE MONEYBAGS HAS POSTED ANOTHER VIDEO ON NEWTUBE.

SHE'S SO COOL!

THAT'S IT!

BLEEP! BLEEP! BLEEP! BLEEP!

VLOGGERS EARN LOADS OF MONEY! FUDGIE, WE'RE GOING TO MAKE YOU A NEWTUBE STAR!

BUT MY MUM'S CRUMMY OLD MOBILE DOESN'T HAVE A GOOD CAMERA!

I KNOW EXACTLY WHERE TO GET A DECENT MOBILE!

LATER, AT MINNIE'S HOUSE...

DAD... I NEED YOU TO DO THE WASHING UP!

ERM... IS THAT MY PHONE RINGING? I'D BETTER ANSWER IT.

ER... HELLO? MINNIE'S DAD SPEAKING.

NICE TRY, WISE GUY.

B-BUT THIS ISN'T MY MOBILE. WHAT HAPPENED TO MY WHIZZ-PHONE X?

I'LL GIVE YOU THREE GUESSES! – ED

RIGHT, I'VE GOT DAD'S SWANKY NEW PHONE. NOW TO GIVE YOU A MAKEOVER! ALL THE MOST SUCCESSFUL VLOGGERS ARE MEGA-STYLISH!

A CHARITY SHOP

ANOTHER CHARITY SHOP

OPEN

THEN WHY ARE WE GOING INTO A CHARITY SHOP?

ONE QUICK CHANGE LATER...

SEE – I KNEW THEY'D SWAP YOUR BORING OLD CLOTHES FOR ALL THIS WEIRD GEAR! YOU LOOK FANTASTIC!

ARE YOU SURE? I DON'T THINK MY MUM'S GOING TO BE VERY HAPPY.

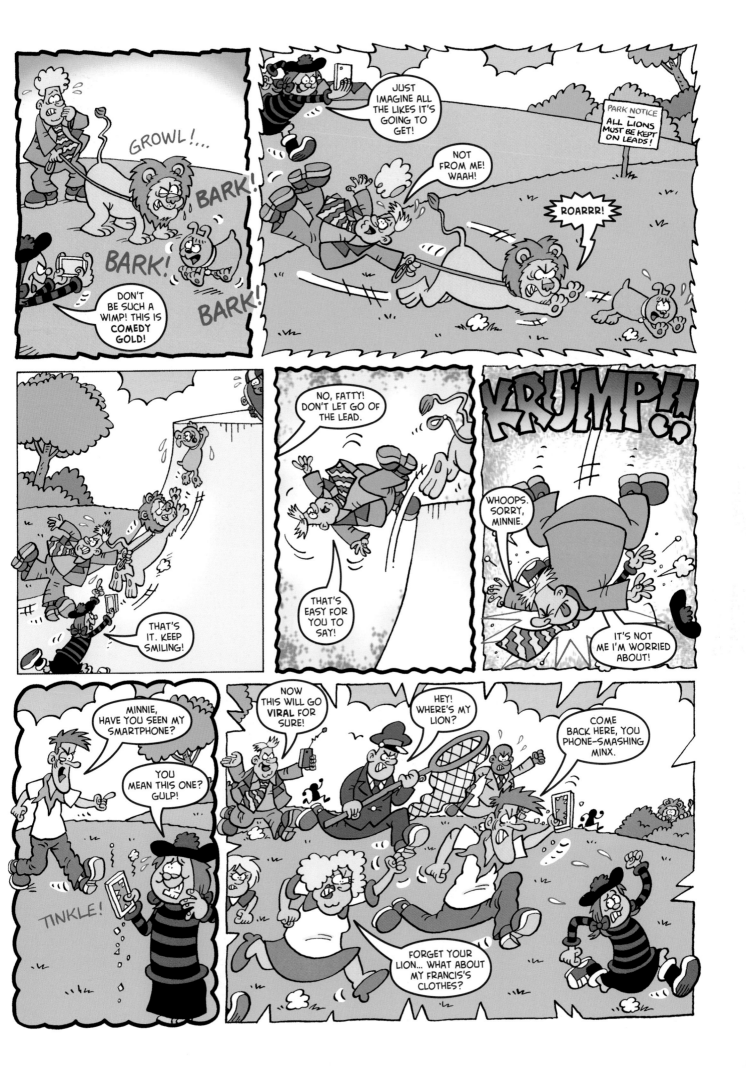

BETTY AND THE YETI!

THE ORDINARY GIRL WITH THE EXTRAORDINARY BEST FRIEND!

THERE WE GO! THAT SHOULD STOP YOU RUNNING OFF!

GRUNT!

GASP! ICE CREAM VAN!

WHAT DID I JUST SAY? NO RUNNING...

...OFF!

YETI! STOP!

YUCK!

GOOD AFTERNOON, SIR!

TWO UNI-CONES, PLEASE.

Just Ice For All

Mind that child!

BEEP! BEEP!

GASP! PRINCESS PONY ON TELLY!

UH-OH.

LOVELY WEATHER TODAY, ISN'T IT?

BLEURGH!

I SHOULD NEVER HAVE GIVEN HIM THAT WATCH!

EVENTUALLY...

SIX PRINCESS PONIES ON A MISSION TO SAVE CUPCAKE CANYON...

SIGH. WHY CAN'T I JUST HAVE A CHIHUAHUA LIKE A NORMAL PERSON?

DENNIS & GNASHER

WHERE'S GNASHER?

GNASHER!

WHERE IS HE?

NIGEL PARKINSON.

DENNIS GETS A CALL...

YELLOW?

HELLO, DENNIS. WOULD YOU LIKE TO SEE YOUR DOG AGAIN?

GIVE ME BACK MY DOG, WALTER!

I'M NOT WALTER! YOU CAN'T TELL WHO I AM BECAUSE I'M SPEAKING INTO A VOICE CHANGER!

NO-ONE ELSE WOULD KIDNAP MY DOG!

I COULD BE ANYONE! I COULD TURN OUT TO BE, ER... PLUG!

PLUG?

OR DANNY. OR ANYONE - BECAUSE OF THE VOICE CHANGER!

YEAH, BUT YOU'RE WALTER THOUGH!

WHY HAVE YOU ALWAYS GOT TO RUIN EVERYTHING?!

GNASH! GNASH!

VOICE CHANGER

HOW DID YOU CAPTURE GNASHER?

AH, THAT WOULD BE TELLING! LET'S JUST SAY I...

DID YOU JUST WAVE A SAUSAGE AT HIM?

STOP RUINING EVERYTHING!

WHAT DO YOU WANT?

IF YOU WANT TO SEE YOUR DOG AGAIN, TAKE YOUR ENTIRE LIFE SAVINGS TO THE FALLEN TREE IN THE WOODS! HA-HA!

GNASH! GNASH!

SEE! YOU'RE RUINING IT AGAIN! YOU'RE MEANT TO BE ALL LIKE 'NO! NOT MY LIFE SAVINGS!'

YEAH, OKAY.

DO YOU WANT MY LIFE SAVINGS OR NOT?!

JUST BE THERE!

HOW DO YOU COPE BEING AROUND HIM ALL THE TIME?!

YOU GET USED TO HIM.

GNASH! GNASH!

HE ALWAYS RUINS EVERYTHING! DO YOU REMEMBER WHEN I SWAPPED HIS HOMEWORK FOR A FAKE HOMEWORK I MADE?

HA-HA!

I'LL MAKE IT EXTRA MESSY AND SMUDGY AND CREASED AND EVEN SPELL DENNIS WITH ONE 'N'!

SCRIBBLE

MIS-SPELL

SCRAWL

BLOT

SCRATCH

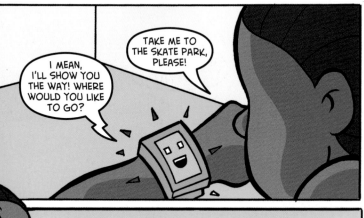

ROGER THE DODGER
HE'S ALWAYS GOT A TRICK UP HIS SLEEVE!

AT BEANOTOWN BEACH...

MUM, CAN WE HAVE SOME MONEY FOR ICE CREAM?

WHERE'S THE MONEY WE GAVE YOU EARLIER?

IT'S GONE. AN ANGRY SEAGULL FLEW DOWN AND STOLE IT FROM US!

MONEY GRABBING SEAGULLS?

IS THIS TRUE?

ARRGH! NO! ROGER AND I SPENT IT ALL AT THE ARCADE.

DAVE!

NO MORE MONEY FOR YOU TWO.

WE NEED TO WHIP UP A DODGE.

SANDCASTLE COMPETITION FIRST PRIZE £50

DAVE, ARE YOU THINKING WHAT I'M THINKING?

CRUNCHER KERR!

NO! I WASN'T THINKING ABOUT HIM, I WAS THINKING WE SHOULD ENTER THE COMPETITION.

NO! CRUNCHER IS HERE TOO.

YOU DON'T STAND A CHANCE AGAINST ME. I'M THE SANDCASTLE MASTER.

YOU HAVE 30 MINUTES. THE BEST CASTLE WINS THE PRIZE MONEY.

GO!

SO...

LEFT A BIT. RIGHT A BIT.

THIS WOULD BE EASIER IF YOU HELPED DIG!

BEANO

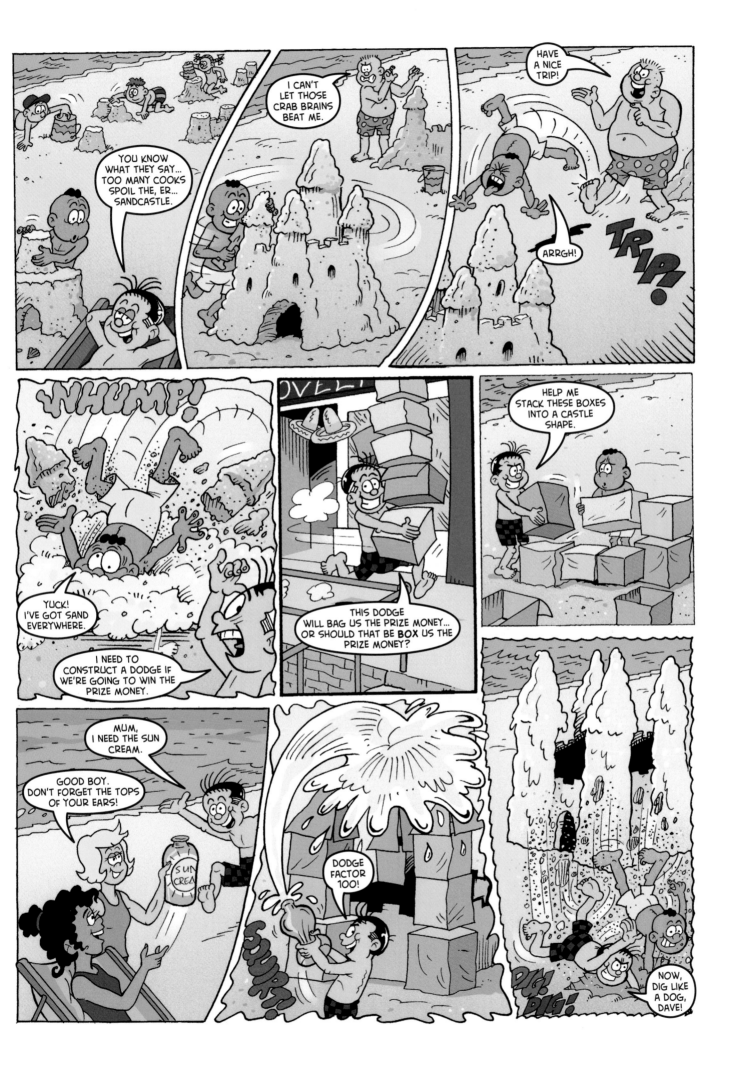

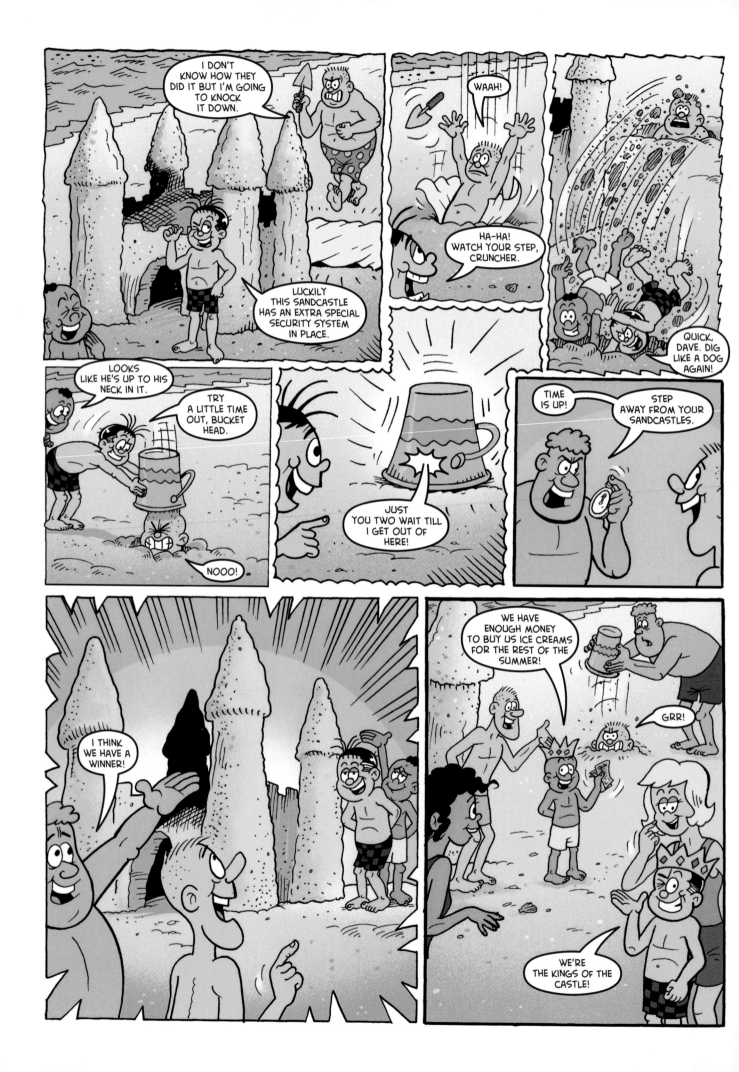

THE BASH STREET KIDS

THE CLASS EVERY TEACHER DREADS...

ONE DAY...

THAT'S THE ENTIRE SCHOOL REDECORATED, INSIDE AND OUT!

DAZZLE!

VROOM!

PAINTERS AND DECORATORS

IT'S JUST A SHAME WE COULDN'T GET THE OUTER WALL PAINTED, TOO. THERE WASN'T ENOUGH MONEY LEFT IN THE BUDGET.

BUT I MAY HAVE A PLAN FOR THAT.

Cuthbert is a swot!

2B rulez

Danny is the BOSS

Plug is handsome signed Plug

Fatty is slim

SOON...

YOU CAN COVER THE OUTER WALL WITH A COLOURFUL MURAL!

GROAN!

Plug is hand Sign

2B rulez

Danny is the BOSS

PAIN PAIN PAINT

I WANT YOU TO PAINT SOMETHING BRIGHT AND FRESH THAT REFLECTS THE TRUE ATMOSPHERE OF BASH STREET SCHOOL.

COME ON, GANG – THE SOONER WE START, THE SOONER WE'LL FINISH.

NNGH!

STIR! TUG!

PAI PAIN INT

PHEW! IT'S OPEN.

HEY! YOU SPLASHED PAINT ON ME!

OPEN! TWANG!

PAINT PAINT

SPLOT!

TAKE THAT!

FLIP!

PAINT

SPLOT! PA

MISSED!

A MASSIVE PAINT BATTLE ENSUES...

GERROFF!

SPLISH!

SPLASH!

SPLASH!

SPLOT!

SPLASH!

GRR!

SOON...

I CAN'T LEAVE YOU ALONE FOR FIVE MINUTES! SCRUB THAT WALL, THEN GET CLEANED UP AND START ALL OVER AGAIN! AND I'LL BE WATCHING!

BUT IT LOOKS GREAT!

LEAP BACK!

I NEVER THOUGHT I'D SAY THIS, BUT I'D PREFER TO DO ACTUAL SCHOOL WORK.

SCRUB! SCRUB!

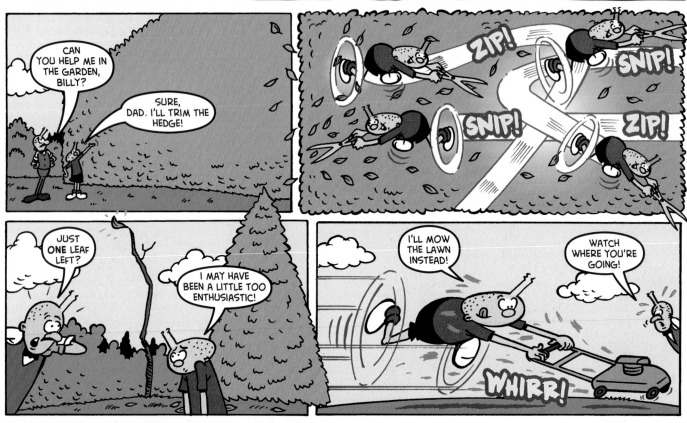

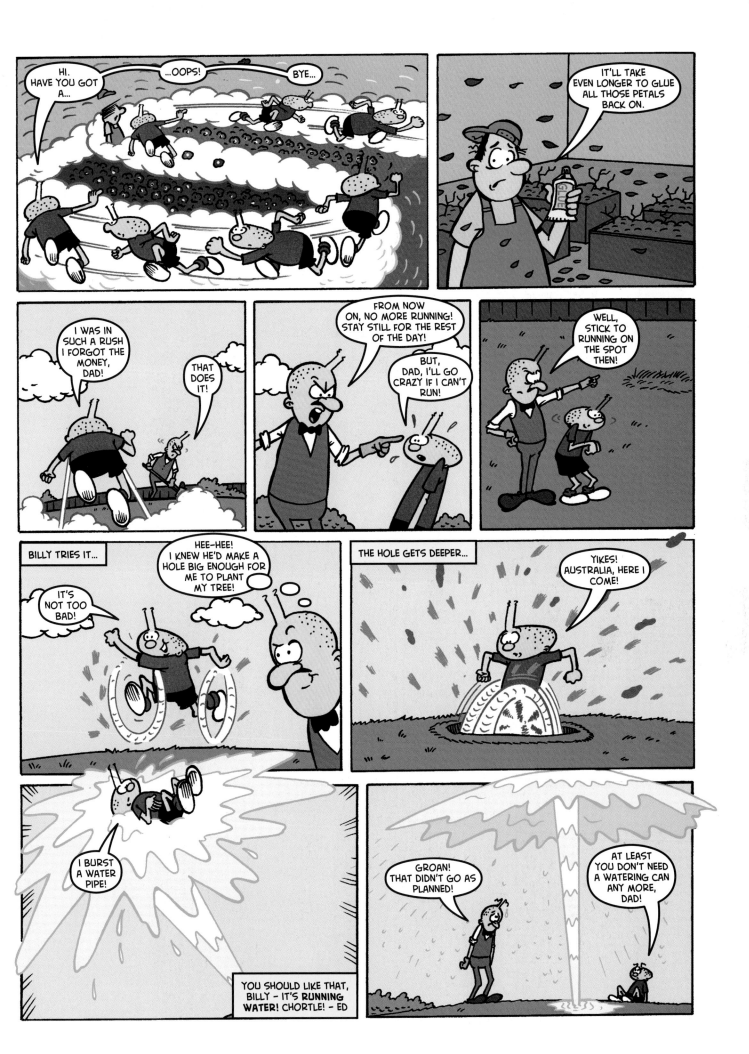

RUBI'S SCREWTOP SCIENCE

THANKS TO RUBI'S NEW INVENTION, THE DIMENSION JUMPER, RUBI AND PIE FACE ARE JUMPING FROM DIMENSION TO DIMENSION, HOPING EACH TIME THAT THEIR NEXT JUMP WILL BE THEIR JUMP HOME...

HERE WE GO AGAIN!

PAFF!

SO FAR, SO NORMAL.

LET'S WAIT UNTIL WE'VE LOOKED OUTSIDE.

THERE'S MINNIE, BACK TO HER REGULAR SELF!

OH YES! PHEW! MAYBE WE DID MAKE IT HOME THIS TIME!

ZOOM

COME BACK HERE, MINNIE! IT'S DINNER TIME!

?!

KID FOOD

COME BACK HERE NOW! BAD GIRL!

THAT WAS... UNUSUAL.

AND IT'S GETTING MORE, ER... UNUSUALER!

KID FOOD

WHOA! THIS PLACE REALLY HAS GONE TO THE DOGS!

HEY, DANNY! NO PULLING!

THIS IS TOO WEIRD!

WE MUST HAVE COME TO A DIMENSION WHERE PEOPLE ARE THE PETS AND PETS ARE THE PEOPLE!

HUMANS MUST BE KEPT ON A LEASH AT ALL TIMES

DOES THAT MEAN WE'RE PETS NOW?

DOG

Diary of a Prankster

By Tricky Dicky aged 8¼

PRANK No. 2

YOU'LL NEED:
- Plastic cups
- Plastic spiders

Dear Diary,
What's nicer than a lovely cup of – SPIDERS?!
This prank will put anyone into a spin!

1 Fill the cups with your plastic spiders.

2 Open the door so there is a small gap.

3 Balance the cups above the door.

ARRGH!

4 When someone comes through the door, it will be RAINING SPIDERS!

I AM SLEEPY... SLEEEEPY...

THAT'S BETTER.

YOU'RE NOW THE MEANEST AND NASTIEST CROOK IN BEANOTOWN.

I AM THE MEANEST, NASTIEST CROOK?

I'M MEAN AND NASTY!

ISN'T HE LOVELY AND HORRIBLE?

I'M NOT SURE. I DON'T TRUST HIM. WE NEED TO TEST HIM.

WHERE'S HE GONE?

HE'S BEEN PINCHING CANDY FROM A BABY.

HE'S STARTING WITH THE CLASSICS.

IT WORKED! HE'S A FOUL VILLAIN.

HERE'S THE PLAN. THERE ARE ANCIENT TUNNELS UNDER BASH STREET SCHOOL WHICH ARE BOUND TO BE FULL OF GOLD AND DIAMONDS.

WE'RE GOING TO ROB THOSE TUNNELS.

I LIKE THE PLAN BUT IT NEEDS JUST ONE LITTLE CHANGE.

WHAT KIND OF CHANGE?

YOU'RE FIRED. I'M STEALING THE GOLD AND DIAMONDS!

YOU'RE RIGHT. HE REALLY IS MEAN, ROTTEN AND NASTY.

LET'S GO BACK TO DANDYTOWN WHERE IT'S SAFER!

TIME FOR SCHOOL TO BE OUT FOREVER!

BOO TO SCHOOL.

DON'T WORRY, MINNIE...

...THERE'S NO SCHOOL TODAY.

I WISH THERE WAS NO SCHOOL TODAY.

NO, I MEAN THERE'S NO SCHOOL. IT'S GONE!

WHAT?!

IT'S GONE?!

YAY!

THIS IS THE HAPPIEST DAY OF MY LIFE!

NO MORE SCHOOL!

BANANAMAN! YOU'RE OUR HERO!

SCHOOL MAY BE GONE...

...BUT THERE ARE SOME NICE TUNNELS FOR YOU ALL TO WORK IN, DIGGING FOR MY GOLD AND DIAMONDS.

DID HE USE THE 'W' WORD?

HE DEFINITELY SAID 'WORK'.

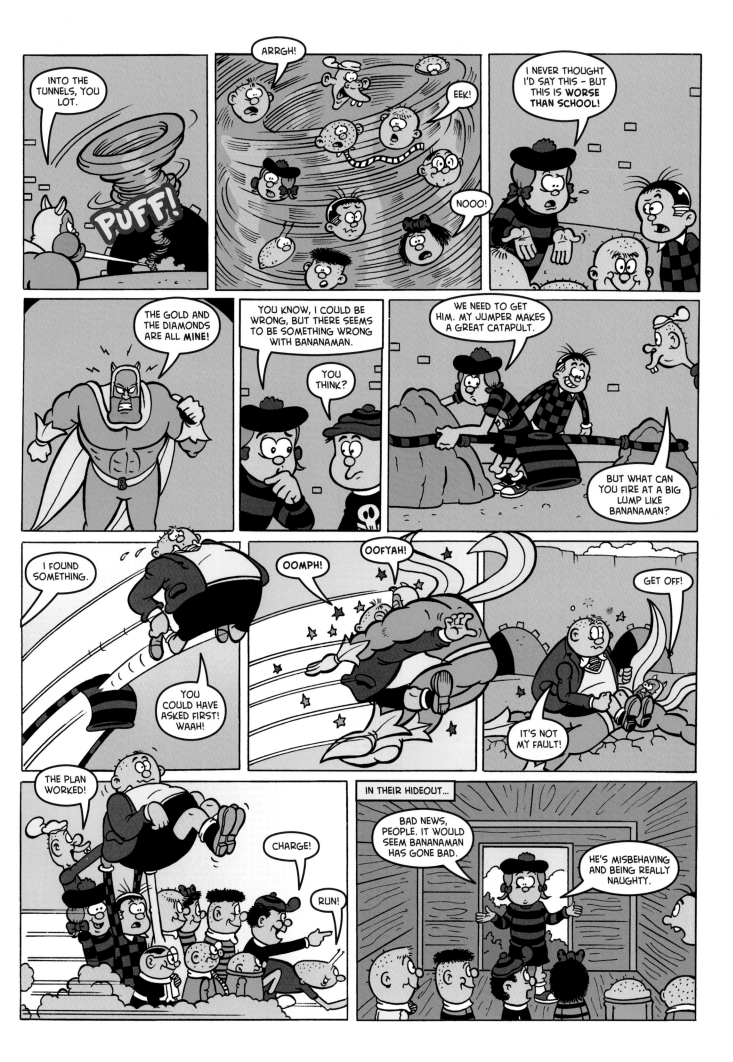

AND THAT'S OUR JOB!

EXACTLY.

WE NEED TO SORT THIS OUT. WE HAVE TO CAPTURE BANANAMAN.

HOW DO WE DO THAT EXACTLY?

DO I HAVE TO DO EVERYTHING? SNEAKY STUFF IS YOUR DEPARTMENT.

IT SOUNDS LIKE A LOT OF WORK.

UNLESS YOU THINK YOU **CAN'T**, OF COURSE.

OOH. THAT'S FIGHTING TALK!

I KNOW WHAT YOU'RE DOING. YOU'RE TRYING TO MAKE ME DETERMINED TO PROVE I CAN.

WELL, IT WON'T WORK. IT WON'T, IT WON'T, IT WON'T!

YOU'RE RIGHT – HE COULDN'T THINK OF ANYTHING.

OH, ALL RIGHT, YOU WIN. I'LL THINK OF SOMETHING.

HMMM... MAYBE IF WE DO THIS... AND A BIT OF THAT...

...GOT IT!

WE NEED TWO VOLUNTEERS TO LURE THE BIG BLUE MUG IN.

ARE YOU SURE SENDING THOSE TWO IS THE BEST IDEA? I MEAN, IT'S SMIFFY AND 'ERBERT!

DID YOU SAY SMIFFY AND 'ERBERT?!

OKAY, MAYBE THAT WASN'T MY BEST IDEA.

GOOD MORNING, MADAM.

IT'S NO GOOD. I CAN'T SEE A BLUE MUG ANYWHERE!

I'VE SPOTTED TWO OF THE LITTLE MOLES WHO ESCAPED FROM THE TUNNELS. I'LL GET THEM BACK TO WORK.

HEY, YOU TWO! THIS WAY – QUICK!

WHAT WAY?

THERE'S NO ESCAPE FROM ME – I'M THE WORST OF THE BUNCH!

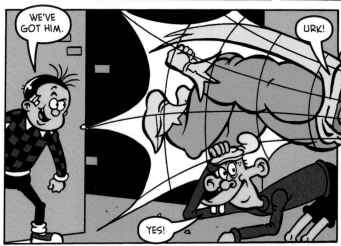

WE'VE GOT HIM.

URK!

YES!

NOOOO!

GRAB THE NET!

OKAY, WE'VE GOT IT!

YOU'RE WRONG – IT'S GOT US!

NOW WHAT?!

HOLD ON! WE'RE TAKING OFF!

NO WE'RE NOT, HE'S DOWN.

OOFYAH!

I'M FEELING PRETTY DOWN MYSELF AFTER ALL OF THAT.

HIS EYES ARE ALL WEIRD – IT LOOKS LIKE HE'S BEEN HYPNOTISED.

BUY THE DANDY ANNUAL 2020 TO FIND OUT WHAT HAPPENED TO BANANAMAN ON HIS HOLIDAY TO DANDYTOWN.

MINNIE THE MINX
SHE'S TOUGHER THAN ALL THE BOYS...

BILLY WHIZZ
THE FASTEST BOY IN THE WORLD!

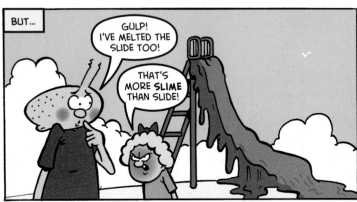

NOPE, NO DIFFERENCE! – ED

ANOTHER KEYBOARD RUINED!

UH-OH! HE'S GOING INTO MELTDOWN!

I'LL TAKE IT TO BEANOTOWN DUMP FOR YOU, MR QUAVER!

ZOOM!

LOCAL ART GALLERY OWNER!

WHAT A MASTERPIECE! THIS SCULPTURE SPEAKS TO MY VERY SOUL!

THIS GUY THINKS IT'S A WORK OF ART!

SOON...

HE'S PUT ON AN EXHIBITION OF MY 'WORK'!

REMARKABLE!

SHEER GENIUS!

PLUG DESCENDING A STAIRCASE

£150

£30

NOCTURNE IN BEANOTOWN

£50

ARTIST'S FATHER

I MADE SOME FAST MONEY THERE!

YOU CAN USE IT TO REPLACE THE STUFF YOU RUINED!

SIGH! NOW IT'S ALL ABOUT TO MELT AWAY!

Diary of a Prankster

By Tricky Dicky aged 8¼

PRANK No. 3

Dear Diary,
This prank will really burst your friend's bubble!

1 First, pinch your friend's shoes.

2 Cut the bubble wrap the same width as the sole of the shoe.

3 Stick the bubble wrap to the soles and put the shoes back where you found them

4 When they put them on, they won't know where the weird popping noise is coming from!

BETTY AND THE YETI!

THE ORDINARY GIRL WITH THE EXTRAORDINARY BEST FRIEND!

HR

DANGEROUS DAN!
BEANOTOWN'S TOP SECRET AGENT!

GROAN! MY **LEAST** FAVOURITE JOB...

...IS WALKING ALL OUR SECRET AGENT DOGS SO THEY CAN DO THEIR 'SPY BUSINESS'.

YAP! YAP! YAP! YAP! YAP! YAP! YAP!

BLIMEY! FOR SUPER-TRAINED, HIGHLY DISCIPLINED, ACROBATIC, KARATE EXPERT CANINE SIDEKICKS, THEY'RE **TOTALLY** OUT OF CONTROL!

YANK!

UNLESS I USE THEIR SPY TRAINING IN MY FAVOUR!

SO...

ATTEN-SHUN!

FORMATION FOXTROT TANGO BEANO CHARLIE DELTA... NOW!

THAT'S BETTER!

I NEED A WEE.

UH-OH...

RUBI'S SCREWTOP SCIENCE

URRGH! ALL THIS DIMENSION JUMPING IS MAKING ME FEEL QUEASY, RUBI.

I HEAR YOU, PIE FACE!

I THOUGHT YOU SAID YOU FELT QUEASY?

YEAH, BUT PIE MAKES EVERYTHING BETTER! CHOMP!

WE NEED TO FIGURE OUT WHERE WE ARE.

RUBI... I THINK YOU NEED TO SEE THIS!

WHEN DID YOU HAVE THESE BILLBOARDS PUT UP?

RUBI IS WATCHING YOU

I DIDN'T, PIE FACE! THAT'S NOT ME! I MEAN, IT'S ME, BUT IT MUST BE A PARALLEL ME!

HALT, IN THE NAME OF RUBI VON SCREWTOP! ASSAULT OF DRONES WILL NOT BE TOLERATED!

NOT A CHANCE, YOU TIN TWIT!

LOOK, IT'S MINNIE!

DRONE RAY ACTIVATED!

NNNNGGGGH!

OH NO!

ALL... HAIL... RUBI VON SCREWTOP! SHE IS OUR GLORIOUS LEADER!

SUBJECT NEUTRALISED.

YIKES!

IT LOOKS LIKE IT USED SOME SORT OF MIND-CONTROL RAY.

YOU NEED TO HAVE A WORD WITH YOURSELF!

WATCH

HA-HA! THAT'S PRETTY FUNNY, PIE FACE.

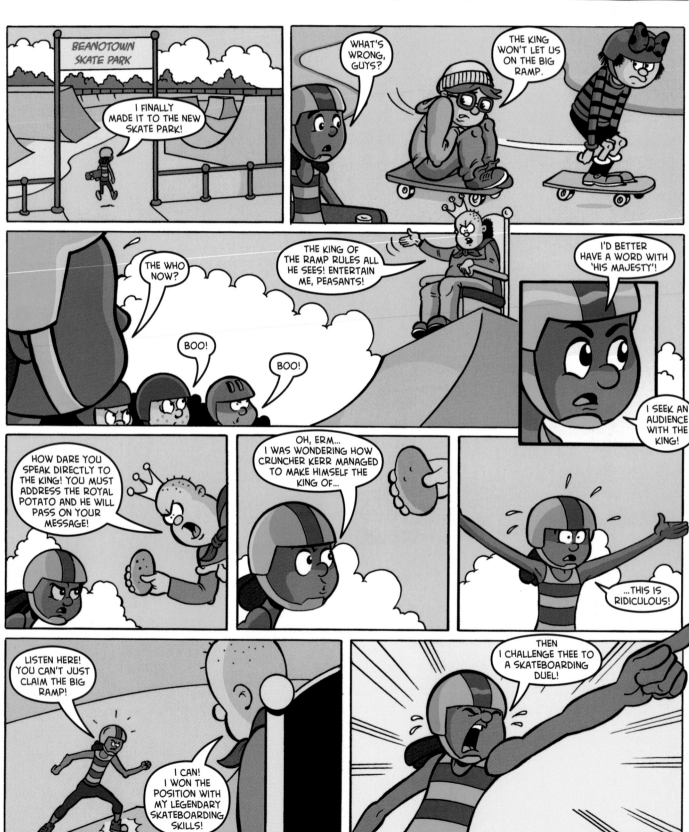

THE CLASS EVERY TEACHER DREADS...
THE BASH STREET KIDS

CLASS 2B IS ON A SCHOOL TRIP...

WE'RE HERE!

AT LAST!

BEANOTOWN FAIR

BASH SCHOOL STREET BUS

SCREECH TO HALT!

REMEMBER, WE'RE ONLY HERE BECAUSE WE'RE BANNED FROM EVERY MUSEUM AND STATELY HOME THAT'S REMOTELY NEAR BEANOTOWN!

THEY FOUND MY HIDDEN STASH OF ULTRA-STICKY JAM TARTS!

STREET BU...

I WANT YOU ALL ON YOUR VERY BEST BEHAVIOUR. YOU ARE REPRESENTATIVES OF BASH STR...

TICKET OFFICE

I'M OFF TO THE HALL OF MIRRORS!

FLATTEN!

...EEK! WHY DO I EVEN BOTHER?

BORIS

BEANOTOWZ FAIR

TEAR!

RIP!

RIP!

CANDY FLOSS!

THE RIFLE RANGE FOR ME!

SHORT BACK AND SIDES, PLEASE.

RIP!

DENNIS & GNASHER

THE WORLD'S WILDEST BOY… AND HIS BEST FRIEND!

THERE'S A WALL AROUND THE TOWN, BUT THAT'S NO REASON NOT TO HAVE A PERFECTLY **NORMAL** ADVENTURE!

RIGHT.

IF WE GO TO THE BEACH, WE CAN SEE IF THERE ARE **PIRATES** ABOUT!

LET'S GO!

DO YOU PREFER REGULAR PIRATES OR ZOMBIE PIRATES?

REALLY OLD ZOMBIE PIRATES BECAUSE… BONES!

ARR! COME BACK WITH MY LEG, YE SCURVY DOG!

AT THE BEACH…

THIS IS WELL WEIRD.

HOW WILL THE PIRATES GET IN?!

LET'S GET A LOLLY.

URRGH! A QUEUE!

LOLLIES AND ICE CREAM COME FROM OUTSIDE THE WALL! I ONLY HAVE **ONE** LEFT!

I'LL GIVE YOU FIVE POUNDS FOR IT!

HEY!

20 POUNDS!

SIX HUNDRED QUID!

A FIGHT BREAKS OUT OVER THE LAST LOLLY…

VA-VOOM!

TO TOWN

THE ICE CREAM VAN IS GETTING AWAY!

AN ANGRY MOB GIVES CHASE…

GIVE US THE LAST LOLLY!

COME ON, GNASHER. TURNS OUT WE DIDN'T NEED PIRATES FOR THE ADVENTURE AFTER ALL!

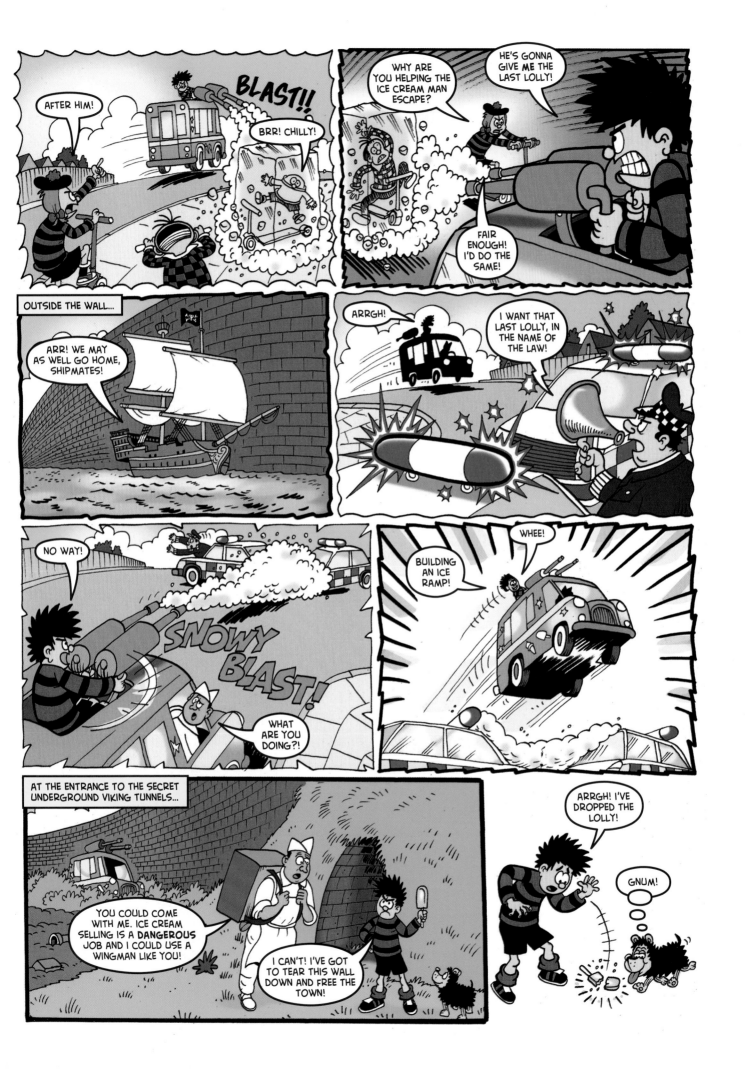

NIGEL PARKINSON.

I THINK YOU'RE LYING!

SMASH!

HA-HA! I'M LOVING BEING KING!

I SAID I'M LOVING BEING KING!

WE HEARD YOU!

AT DENNIS'S DEN...

WHAT ARE WE GOING TO DO ABOUT THE MAYOR'S WALL?

WHAT CAN WE DO? HE'S ALL POWERFUL NOW HE'S KING!

SCAN!

ARRGH!

I'VE SCANNED YOUR FACES BEFORE! IF I SCAN YOU AGAIN, I'LL HAVE YOU LOCKED UP!

ARE YOU PLOTTING AGAINST ME?

EXCUSE ME WHILE I DO AN EVIL LAUGH!

HA! HA! HA! HA! HA! HA! HA! HA! HA! HA!

BUT...

HUH? WHY DID THE DRONE SUDDENLY SHUT DOWN?

CRASH!

ME!

MUM?!

BECAUSE I WORK FOR THE MAYOR, I KNOW THE OVERRIDE CODE FOR THE DRONES!

WHAT'S THE PLAN, MUM?

HOW DO WE BEAT THE MAYOR?

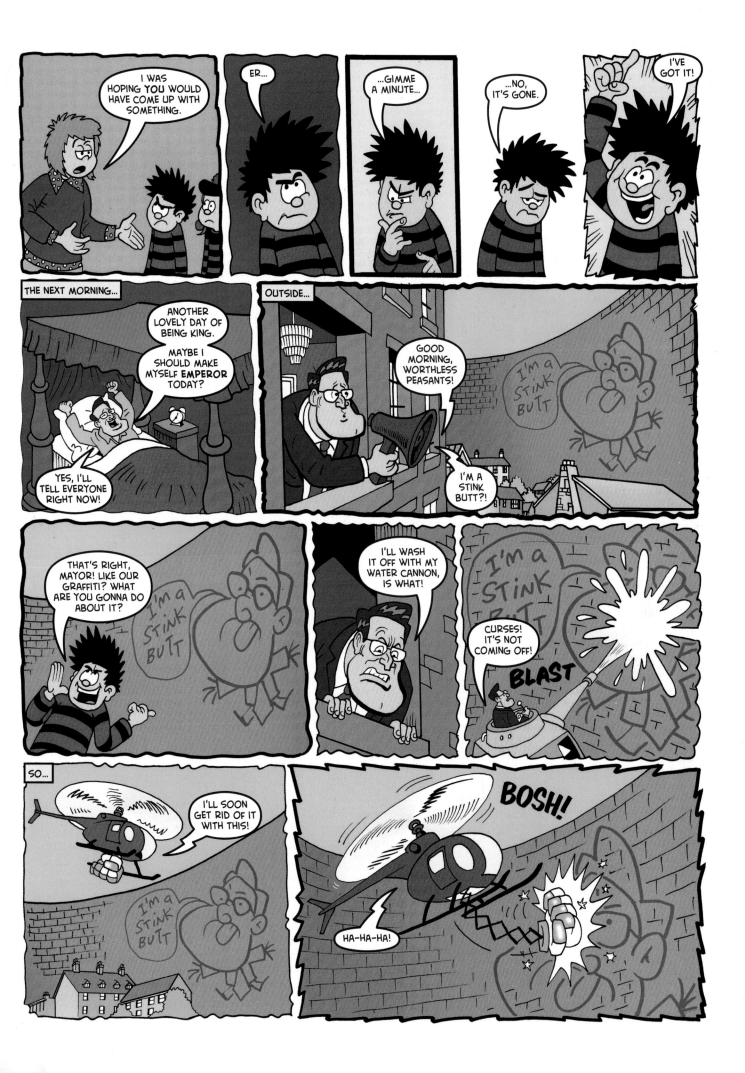

BETTY AND THE YETI!

THE ORDINARY GIRL WITH THE EXTRAORDINARY BEST FRIEND!

TIME FOR YOUR BEDTIME STORY, YETI.

YETI WANT LITTLE RED RIDING HOOD.

ONCE UPON A TIME, THERE WAS A LITTLE GIRL CALLED RED RIDING...

YETI!

OKAY, A YETI CALLED RED RIDING HOOD.

HE WAS ON HIS WAY TO VISIT HIS GRANDMA AT THE OTHER SIDE OF THE WOODS WITH A BASKET OF...

RIDING HOOD EATS BASKET!

FINE! ANYWAY, THERE WAS A MEAN WOLF LURKING IN THE WOODS...

RIDING HOOD EATS WOLF!

OKAY... SO SHE ARRIVED AT GRANDMA'S HOUSE, BUT...

RIDING HOOD EATS GRANDMA!

NO LEAFLETS!

LISTEN, HE CAN'T EAT EVERYTHING! IT'S JUST NOT REALISTIC!

SCOFF!

Fairytales

THE END. BURP!

HR

BILLY WHIZZ
THE FASTEST BOY IN THE WORLD!

A PEACEFUL WINTER'S DAY IN BEANOTOWN. THE SNOW LIES CALMLY ON THE GROUND...

...BUT NOT FOR LONG!

I'VE GOT TO GET TO BEANOTOWN PARK!

ZOOM!

YIKES! A SUDDEN BLIZZARD!

GLUB!

THE COUNCIL HAS ASKED ME TO TEST THE NEW ROUNDABOUT AFTER I WORE OUT THE LAST ONE!

SEEMS QUITE STURDY!

I'LL GET IT SPINNING AT A GOOD SPEED!

SPIN!

UH-OH! IT'S UPROOTED ITSELF!

THAT CAN'T BE GOOD.

THE ROUNDABOUT PASSES THROUGH TOWN...

ARRGH! A TORNADO!

I'D BETTER TRY TO CATCH IT!

OO-ER! LISTEN TO THAT THUNDER! THERE MUST BE A MEGASTORM COMING NEXT!

SONIC BOOM!

NOPE, IT'S JUST BILLY BREAKING THE SOUND BARRIER! - ED

THE TORNADO CIRCLES BACK TO BEANOTOWN PARK...

GASP! THERE'S A BIG WHIRLPOOL IN THE BOATING LAKE!

THERE'S NO SIGN OF THE ROUNDABOUT ANYWHERE. I MIGHT AS WELL WHIZZ HOME!

ERM... I THINK IT ENDED UP IN THE BOATING LAKE, BILLY! - ED

BACK HOME...

MY FEET ARE RED-HOT AFTER ALL THAT RUNNING! I'LL COOL THEM DOWN IN THE SNOW!

MUCH BETTER!

WOW! BILLY'S FEET ARE HOT ENOUGH TO MELT ALL THE SNOW! - ED

OH NO! A FLOOD!

GROO! SOGGY SOCKS!

BUT AT BILLY'S HOUSE...

EXTREME WEATHER HIT BEANOTOWN TODAY WITH A BLIZZARD, A TORNADO, SEVERE THUNDER AND FLOODING!

NEWS

WHAT'S HE ON ABOUT?! THE WEATHER'S BEEN PERFECTLY NORMAL ALL DAY! FAKE NEWS!

DANGEROUS DAN!
BEANOTOWN'S TOP SECRET AGENT!

OH NO! WE WENT TO AN EVIL PARALLEL UNIVERSE AND NOW THE EVIL RUBI HAS STOLEN THE DIMENSION JUMPER AND VANISHED, LEAVING US TRAPPED HERE!

I KNOW, PIE FACE. I WAS WITH YOU.

I THOUGHT I'D JUST GO OVER IT ALL AGAIN, IN CASE ANYONE FORGOT.

LIKE WHO? AND WHY ARE YOU WINKING AT ME?

I GRABBED A LOOSE THREAD FROM THE JUMPER BEFORE EVIL ME DISAPPEARED! GRAB MY HAND!

YOU'RE **THREADY** FOR ANYTHING, RUBI!

I WONDER IF WE'LL END UP IN A PARALLEL UNIVERSE WHERE YOUR PUNS ARE BETTER?

PAFF!

A PUN-IVERSE, MORE LIKE!

WHEREVER WE ARE, WE'RE HERE!

EVERYTHING LOOKS NORMAL! I THINK WE FINALLY MADE IT BACK!

HI, RUBI! HI, PIE FACE!

NOW WE FIND THE EVIL ME AND ROBOT YOU.

TIME TO FOLLOW THE THREAD!

SO...

THE TRAIL ENDS AT YOUR LAB. IMAGINE WHAT SHE COULD DO WITH ALL YOUR TECH, RUBI!

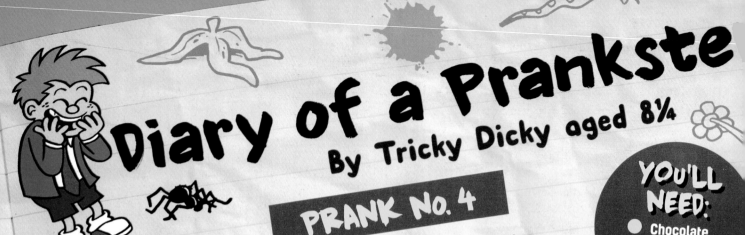

Diary of a Prankste

By Tricky Dicky aged 8¼

PRANK No. 4

YOU'LL NEED:
- Chocolate sandwich cookies
- Toothpaste

Dear Diary,
This prank really takes the COOKIE!

1 Start separating the cookies.

2 With an adult's help, scrape out the filling.

3 Spread the toothpaste over the cookie and sandwich them back together.

4 Dad sure felt crummy when he ate one!

THE BASH STREET KIDS

THE CLASS EVERY TEACHER DREADS...

ONE MORNING...

THE HEAD HAS DECIDED, FOR MANAGING NOT TO COMPLETELY DESTROY THE SCHOOL FOR AN ENTIRE MONTH, THAT YOU SHOULD HAVE A REWARD. I'VE GOT JUST THE THING IN MIND.

BASH SCHOOL STREET BUS

BUT...

BEANOTOWN CRAZY GOLF COURSE

OH DEAR. IT DOESN'T SEEM TO BE OPEN.

BAH!

CLOSED

IF WE KEEP QUIET, MAYBE THOSE AWFUL KIDS FROM BASH STREET SCHOOL WILL GO AWAY!

STREET

BACK AT SCHOOL...

I GUESS WE'LL HAVE TO RESUME OUR LESSONS, ONCE I GET BACK FROM EXPLAINING THE SITUATION TO THE HEAD.

2B

UNEXPECTED REALLY HARD MATHS TEST
Teacher

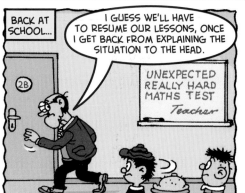

WE SHOULDN'T BE DENIED OUR TREAT JUST BECAUSE THE CRAZY GOLF COURSE WAS CLOSED.

YEAH!

WE'LL BRING THE CRAZY GOLF TO US!

WHAP!

FIRST, WE NEED A GOLF CLUB EACH.

SPRAY STARCH

ANCIENT SCHOOL SUPPLIES

THEN, WE NEED A GOLF BALL. THIS CRUSHED UP MATHS TEST PAPER WILL DO.

THIS OLD SPROUT IS WELL HARD!

CRUSH!

FRESH SCHOOL FRUIT AND VEG.

THE WINNER WILL BE THE FIRST PLAYER TO GET PAST ALL THE OBSTACLES AND GET THEIR BALL INTO TEACHER'S FAVOURITE MUG AT THE SCHOOL GATE.

SWEEP!

PLONK!

SO...

2B

ON YOUR MARKS, GET SET, GOLF!

JJ'S JOKES
BUY ONE, GET FUN FREE!

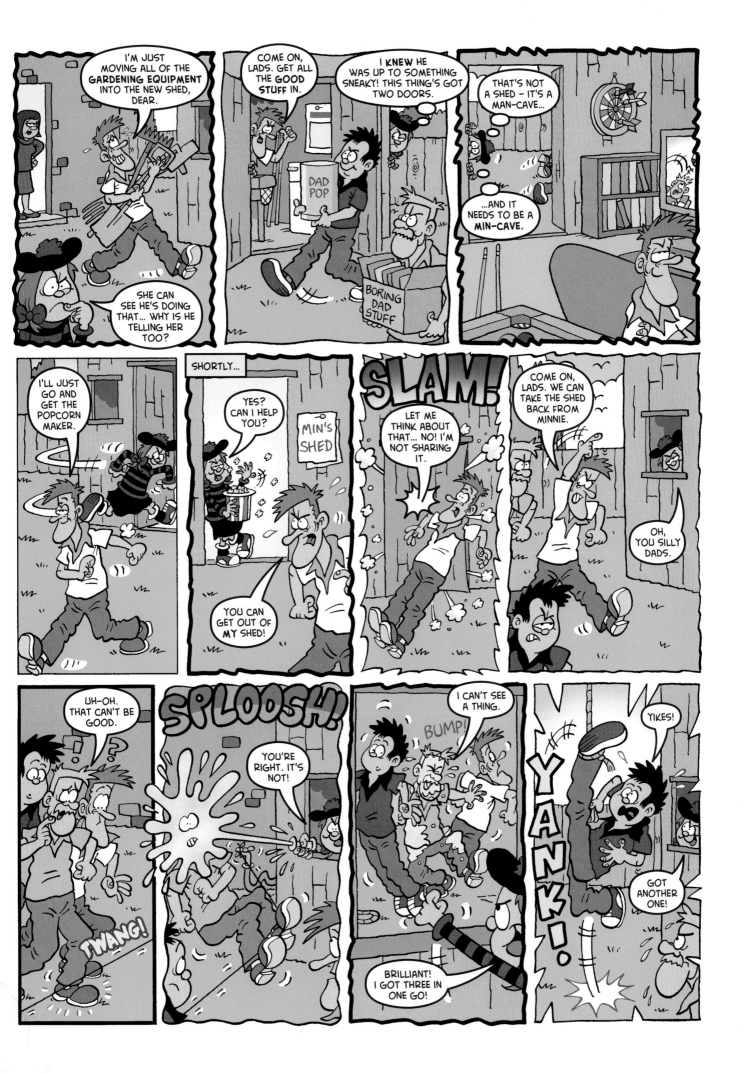

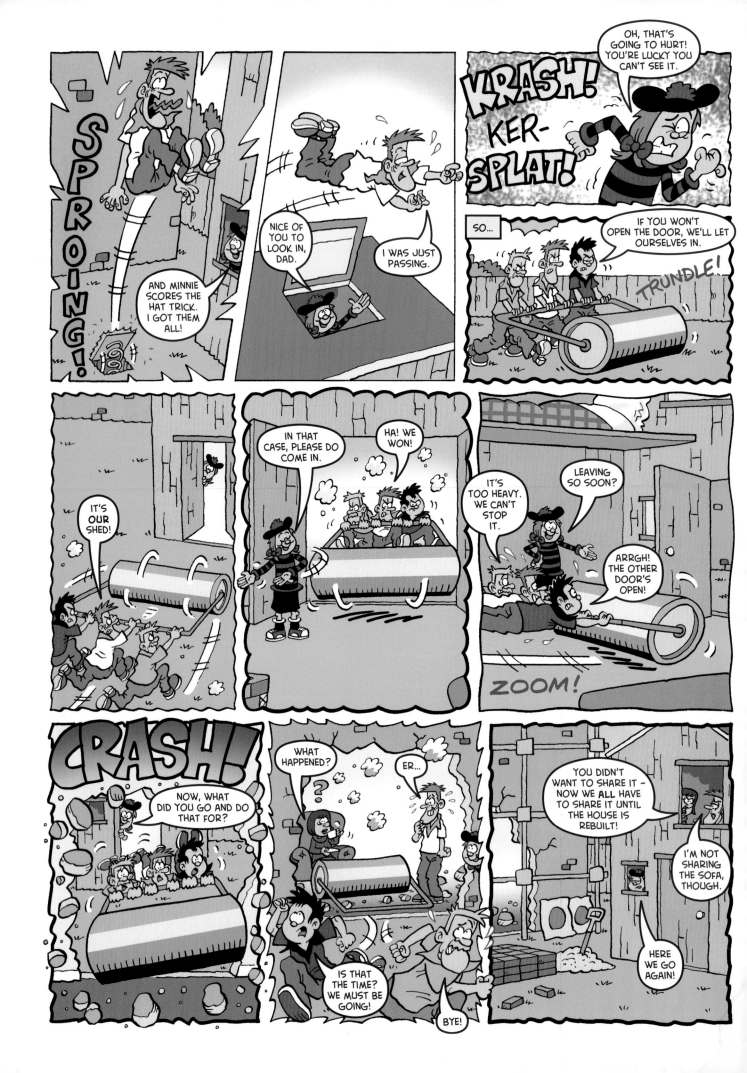

DENNIS & GNASHER

THE MAYOR'S WALL AROUND BEANOTOWN HAS BEEN DEMOLISHED, SO DENNIS AND GNASHER CAN RELAX AT LAST...

THE TOWN IS SAVED! NOW WE CAN CHILL.

NIGEL PARKINSON.

A SECOND LATER...

I'M BORED.

I WISH SOMETHING WOULD HAPPEN.

YOU SHOULD BE CAREFUL WHAT YOU WISH FOR.

SOMETHING WILL HAPPEN GNOW. IT ALWAYS DOES. ANY SECOND GNOW.

GNOW?

PHEW!

MAYBE GNOT TODAY...

HELP, DENNIS!

ELLIS THE ESCAPING ELEPHANT?!

DUDE, YOU GOTTA HIDE ME!

HEAVE!

ARE THE BEANOTOWN ZOOKEEPERS AFTER YOU? DO YOU NEED ME TO HELP YOU HIDE?

HE'S LIKE A TEN YEAR OLD SHERLOCK HOLMES!

HIDE IN THE CUPBOARD UNDER THE STAIRS! THEY'LL NEVER FIND YOU THERE!

SO...

TRY BREATHING IN.

URRGH! IT'S LIKE YOU'RE NOT EVEN TRYING!

LIKE THIS!

WE'LL HIDE YOU UPSTAIRS INSTEAD.

SHOVE!

AND...

SORTED.

BEANO

I'M GNOT GNOT CONVINCED.

SUDDENLY...

WHAT WAS ALL THE BANGING AND CRASHING I HEARD IN HERE?

HANG ON! IS THAT...

PARP

HE'S KNOCKED OUT!

LET'S GET OUT OF HERE BEFORE HE WAKES UP!

DOWNSTAIRS...

WE'LL TRY A DISGUISE.

PUT THIS ON!

YOU MIGHT WANT TO THINK ABOUT LOSING SOME WEIGHT.

EIGHT COATS AND A SOMBRERO LATER...

IF ANYONE LOOKS REALLY CLOSELY, THEY'LL STILL BE ABLE TO TELL IT'S YOU.

I KNOW - SUNGLASSES!